…The Cunas love to dance and sing and have many fun customs. Traditionally, the women embroider pictures of these customs into the brightly colored molas that are part of their shirts...

www.rourkepublishing.com

The Lazy Giant
is based on a Cuna tale
from Panama included
in *Leyendas del Caribe*
by Rafael Morales, 1959

To my love, Shahram
-S.S.

Editor: Frank Sloan

Library of Congress
Cataloging-in-Publication Data

Sepehri, Sandy.
  The lazy giant : based on a Cuna tale / retold by Sandy Sepehri ;
Illustrated by Brian Demeter.
      p. cm. -- (Latin American tales and myths)
  ISBN 1-60044-213-7
  1. Cuna mythology. 2. Cuna Indians--Folklore. 3. Legends--Panama. I.
Demeter, Brian, ill. II. Title. III. Series.

  F1565.2.C8S47 2007
  398.2 --dc22

                            2006014658

Printed in the USA

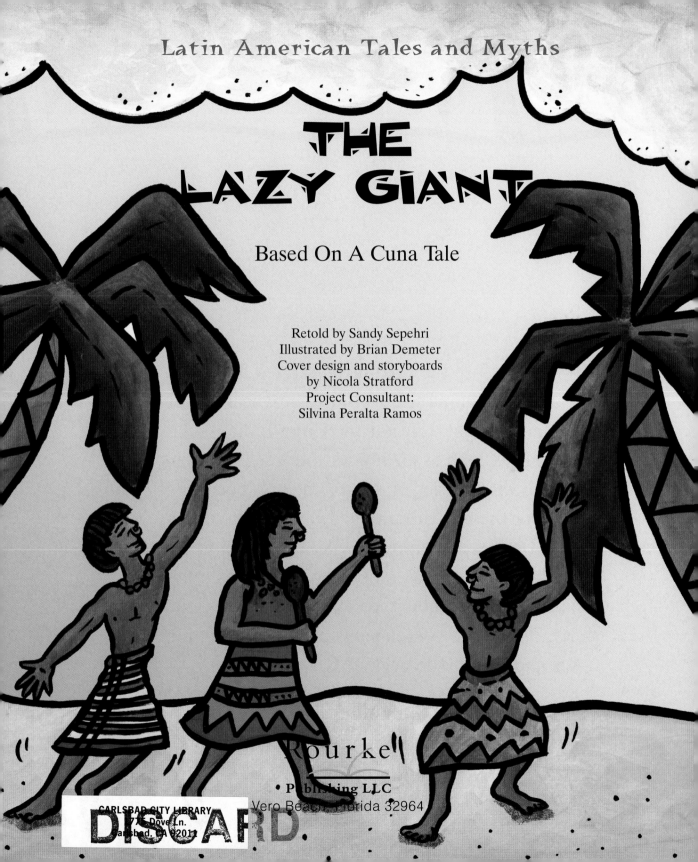

Latin American Tales and Myths

THE LAZY GIANT

Based On A Cuna Tale

Retold by Sandy Sepehri
Illustrated by Brian Demeter
Cover design and storyboards
by Nicola Stratford
Project Consultant:
Silvina Peralta Ramos

Rourke
Publishing LLC
Vero Beach, Florida 32964

Long before the **Spaniards** arrived 500 years ago, the land of **Panama** was as flat as a pancake, without a mountain in sight. Life for the **Cuna** Indians who lived there was as calm as a summer breeze. They planted corn and wild berries on the plain. And because they lived near the sea, there was always plenty of fish.

The Cuna were happy people who loved to dance and sing. The women embroidered pictures into the brightly colored **molas** they wore as part of their shirts. They wore golden rings pierced through their noses and handmade necklaces.

The Cunas all shared in planting and harvesting their crops. And they also shared their food. When the elderly Cunas became tired, they would rest in hammocks tied between **plantain** trees.

Their homes were built of bamboo shoots and thatched roofs, with the ground as their floor. As many as 20 people could live in one house, but they all got along well. And they thanked the giant god **Paquo Meecho** for his protection and care.

Sadly, a winter storm came one year, and the Cunas suffered terribly. The wind soared across the plain, and ocean waves slapped down upon their crops and homes. No longer was it safe to paddle out to the ocean in their **cayucos** to fish. The land became flooded with water, and soon the children began to cry from hunger.

Every Cuna trudged inland and gathered on a grassy meadow. They lifted their hands to the sky and prayed loudly for Paquo Meecho's help.

Paquo Meecho listened to the Cunas' pleas for help. Because of all his duties, he decided to send his son, **Chiriqui**, to help. Chiriqui was sleeping on a cloud.

"Wake up!" shouted Paquo Meecho, "I have a job for you."

"Let me sleep!" Chiriqui said to his father.

"It is time you got up and took your duties seriously," answered his father.

Chiriqui shook the heavens with his growling and yawning. Finally, he sat up to listen to his father.

"**M**y son," said Paquo Meecho, "the Cunas below will soon starve. It will be easy for you to help them. Now go down, and see what you can do!"

Chiriqui climbed down to Earth, using the clouds as a ladder. Like his father, he too was a giant, so his feet sank into the wet ground until he was up to his ankles in mud.

With great anger, Chiriqui plowed his way through the ruined cornfields. He really wanted to go home to his fluffy cloud. Finally, he came to an area covered in large boulders that looked like mere pebbles to this giant.

"Aha!" he said. "I can roll these rocks to the ocean and make them into a large seawall."

ust as he was trying to move the first boulder, it started to rain again. Not wanting to get wet, he decided to return home by climbing up the cloud ladder.

At the top he was surprised to find his father, who said, "You have accomplished nothing! How can you return home while the poor Cunas' homes are being destroyed?"

"Father, I will build them a seawall, but not while the weather is so miserable. When the rain has stopped, I will return. But, for now, I wish to eat my dinner then return to my cloud. I am tired!"

"You are not tired!" shouted Paquo Meecho. "You are lazy! Go back down and do not return until you have helped the Cunas."

Paquo Meecho grabbed his son by the arm and threw him as hard as he could, back down to the Earth. With the speed of a meteor, Chiriqui came hurtling down, ripping through the clouds.

When he hit the Earth, he broke through the surface. Down, down into the moist earth went Chiriqui, down under the village, and down where no one could see him.

When he finally stopped falling, all was dark. There were no heavenly stars or moon to guide him. Even though he was a giant on Earth, he was afraid and wished he had not disobeyed his father.

Far above Chiriqui strange things were happening. Each time Chiriqui's giant knee came pounding down, the earth above him trembled and shook everything.

"We must have angered Paquo Meecho with our cries for help," said the Cuna chief.

And the Cunas said, "Please forgive us, Paquo Meecho! We will bother you no more."

Paquo Meecho was puzzled. "Where is my lazy giant of a son now? I will go down there and wake him up!"

Meanwhile, Chiriqui was having no luck finding his way out by crawling on his knees. He decided to stand up and continue his search. As he stood, he pushed up the ground, forming mountains above him. Luckily for the Cunas, Chiriqui created an entire mountain range along their shore. These mountains beat the storm waves back to the ocean and the Cunas began to rejoice. "Oh, great Paquo Meecho. We see that you were helping us, after all!"

Paquo Meecho approached the Cuna people carefully, so he wouldn't step on anyone.

"Gentle Cunas," he said, "I have heard your prayers and sent my son, Chiriqui, to help you. Have you seen him?"

22

"No, great one," answered the Cuna chief. "We have not seen your son. But, look, see the great mountains that block the ocean from our land."

Paquo Meecho looked and saw the mountains. So he had been working after all.

"Chiriqui! Where are you, my son?" he shouted.

"Father!" replied Chiriqui. "I am here under the ground. Please help me!"

Paquo Meecho could hear his voice, but he couldn't see him. "Oh, why did I fling him to the ground? What a terrible father I am!"

Chiriqui desperately wanted to see his father. Being alone for so long made him realize how much he loved his family. Would he ever see them again? Would they only remember him for his laziness?

If only he had thought of the needy Cunas. Chiriqui decided to call to his father once more. He used all the force within him.

"Father! Please find me!" Chiriqui screamed with one earth-shaking shout.

The shout was so loud that it created the very first volcano the Cunas had ever seen. Hot lava poured over the volcano top.

Knowing that the lava would kill the Cunas, Paquo Meecho laid his hands on the ground and directed the people to climb on them.

nce the volcano
had quieted down, Paquo
Meecho set the villagers down
where the lava had not traveled.
Then he peered inside the volcano.
Chiriqui could see his father's face and
shot up his hand. Paquo Meecho grasped
Chiriqui's wrist and pulled his son out of the volcano.

"My son, I see that you have helped these people. I
am so proud of you."

Chiriqui answered. "My only accomplishment was to
fall through the earth. I must have made these
mountains while I was looking for a way out."

Paquo Meecho said, "I have also discovered
darkness—the darkness that filled my heart when I
could not find you."

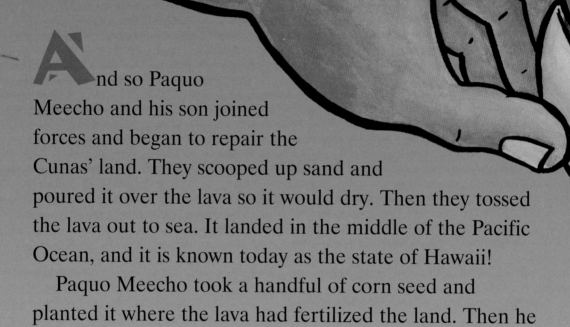

nd so Paquo Meecho and his son joined forces and began to repair the Cunas' land. They scooped up sand and poured it over the lava so it would dry. Then they tossed the lava out to sea. It landed in the middle of the Pacific Ocean, and it is known today as the state of Hawaii!

Paquo Meecho took a handful of corn seed and planted it where the lava had fertilized the land. Then he took out more seeds: sugarcane, rice, oranges, plantains, bananas, and coconuts. When he was done, he watered them all.

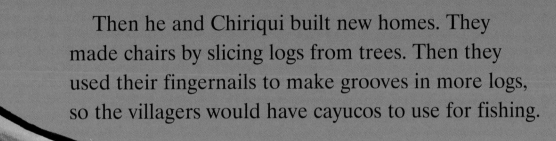

Then he and Chiriqui built new homes. They made chairs by slicing logs from trees. Then they used their fingernails to make grooves in more logs, so the villagers would have cayucos to use for fishing.

The Cunas exhausted themselves thanking Paquo
Meecho and Chiriqui. Then the two said good-bye to
the Cunas and climbed their way back home.
   Exhausted, both Paquo Meecho and Chiriqui flopped
onto their soft clouds and fell instantly to sleep.

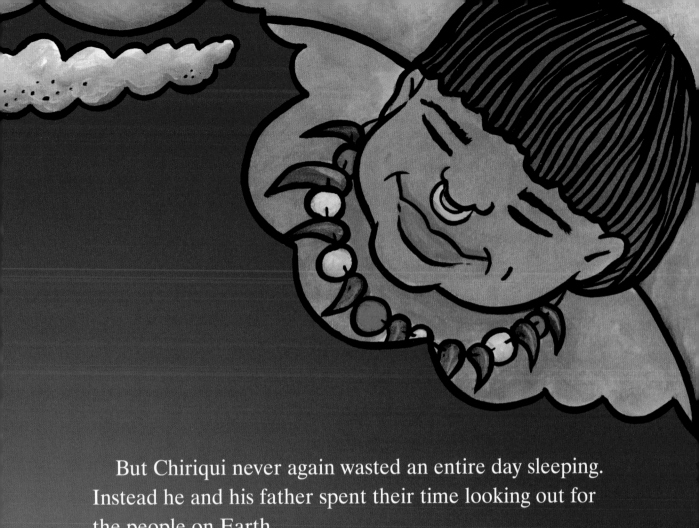

But Chiriqui never again wasted an entire day sleeping. Instead he and his father spent their time looking out for the people on Earth.

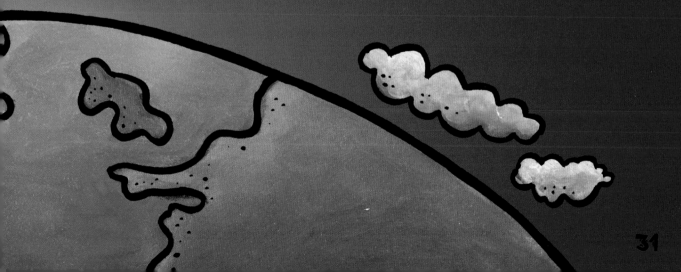

GLOSSARY

cayucos (Kie YOU cose) - canoe made from dugout tree logs, used by the Cunas and other Native American tribes

Chiriqui (CHEER eh kwee) - the highest volcano in the vicinity of the Panama Canal, 3.475 meters above sea level. The volcano was originally named Chiriqui and is now named Baru.

Cuna (KOO nah) - the Cuna Indians are a strongly-knit tribal society living on a chain of islands called San Blas Archipelago, on the Atlantic side of the Republic of Panama

molas (moe LAS) – the Cuna name for their decorative designs sewn on cloth, either geometric, of animals or birds, village scenes, or religious themes

Panama (PAN a ma) – a nation in Central America, bordering both the Caribbean Sea and the North Pacific Ocean, between Colombia and Costa Rica.

Paquo Meecho (PA kuo MEE choe) - the god worshipped in the jungles of Panama 400 years ago who promised revenge against the Spanish conquistadors who invaded Panama in 1517, searching for gold.

plantain (plan TANE) – a banana like tropical fruit

Spaniards (span YERDS) – native inhabitants of Spain

ABOUT THE AUTHOR

Sandy Sepehri lives with her husband, Shahram, and their three children in Florida. She has a bachelor's degree and writes freelance articles and children's stories.